Published 2008 by A & C Black Publishers Limited
36 Soho Square, London W1D 3QY
www.acblack.com

ISBN 978-1-4081-0038-7

Copyright text © Christine Moorcroft 2008
Copyright illustrations © Kevin Hopgood 2008
Copyright cover illustration © Piers Baker 2008
Editor: Dodi Beardshaw
Designed by Bob Vickers

The author and publishers would like to thank Ray Barker
and Rifat Siddiqui for their advice in producing this series
of books.

A CIP catalogue record for this book is available from the
British Library.

Printed and bound in Great Britain by Halstan Printing Group,
Amersham, Buckinghamshire.

The author and publishers are grateful for permission to
reproduce the following: p.59 'Out of Sight' by Roger McGough,
from Sky in the Pie (© Roger McGough 1983), reproduced by
permission of PFD (www.pfd.co.uk) on behalf of Roger McGough.
Every effort has been made to trace copyright holders and to
obtain their permission for use of copyright material. The author
and publishers would be pleased to rectify any error or omission
in future editions.

A&C Black uses paper produced with elemental chlorine-free
pulp, harvested from managed sustainable forests.

Introduction

100% Developing Literacy Creating and Shaping Texts is a series of seven photocopiable activity books for developing children's responses to different types of texts and their understanding of the structure and purposes of different types of texts.

The books provide learning activities to support strands 9 and 10 of the literacy objectives of the Primary Framework for Literacy: Creating and shaping texts and Text structure and organisation.

The structure of 100% **Developing Literacy Creating and Shaping Texts Ages 10–11** is designed to complement the objectives of the Primary Framework and include the range of text types suggested in the planning for Year 6. It addresses the following learning objectives from the Primary Framework for Literacy:

9 Creating and shaping texts

- Set their own challenges to extend achievement and experience in writing
- Use different narrative techniques to engage and entertain the reader
- In non-narrative, establish, balance and maintain viewpoints
- Select words and language drawing on their knowledge of literary features and formal and informal writing
- Integrate words, images and sounds imaginatively for different purposes

10 Text structure and organisation

- Use varied structures to shape and organise text coherently
- Use paragraphs to achieve pace and emphasis

The structure of **Developing Literacy Creating and shaping texts Ages 10–11** focuses on the following types of text:

- Narrative (Fiction genres, Extending narrative, Authors and texts, Short story with flashbacks)
- Non-fiction (Biography and autobiography, Journalistic writing, Argument, Formal/impersonal writing)
- Poetry (The power of imagery, Finding a voice).

The activities

Some of the activities can be carried out with the whole class, some are more suitable for small groups and others are for individual work. It is important that the children are encouraged to enjoy novels, stories, plays, films and poetry, and to enjoy and use non-fiction texts – not just to learn about how they are written – and that they have opportunities to listen to, repeat, learn, recite, join in and improvise on poems for enjoyment. Many of the activities can be adapted for use at different levels, to suit the differing levels of attainment of the children; several can be used in different ways as explained in the notes which follow. Some activities have been based on specific texts: others are generic. Some of those based on specific texts can be adapted for use with others. Passages from fiction have been selected to act as 'tasters' to encourage the children to read the rest of the book and others by the same author.

Reading

Most children will be able to carry out the activities independently but a few might need help in reading some of the instructions on the sheets. If so, it is expected that someone will read them to or with them, or explain them, if necessary.

Organisation

The activities require very few resources besides pencils, crayons, scissors and glue. Other materials are specified in the Teachers' notes on the activity pages: for example, fiction, poetry or information books, websites and CD-ROMs.

Extension activities

Most of the activity sheets end with a challenge (*Now try this!*) which reinforces and extends the children's learning. These more challenging activities might be appropriate for only a few children; it is not expected that the whole class should complete them, although many more children might benefit from them with appropriate assistance – possibly as a guided or shared activity. On some pages there is space for the children to complete the extension activities, but others will require a notebook or a separate sheet of paper.

Accompanying CD

The enclosed CD-ROM contains all the activity sheets from the book in a program which allows you to edit them for printing or saving. This means that modifications can be made to further differentiate the activities to suit pupils' needs. See page 12 for further details.

Notes on the activities

Stories and poems featured or suggested in this book and supplementary texts

Fiction genres

Adventure: *The Oxford Book of Adventure Stories* (edited by Joseph Bristow, OUP), *Fearless* (Tim Lott, Walker), *Fight Game* (Kate Wild, Blackwell), *Oranges in No Man's Land* (Elizabeth Laird, Macmillan), *The Lion, the Witch and the Wardrobe,* (C S Lewis, Collins), *Framed* (Frank Cottrell Boyce, Macmillan)

Mystery: *The Haunting* (Margaret Mahy, Puffin), *Skellig* (David Almond, Hodder), *Kit's Wilderness* (David Almond, Hodder), *The Edge Chronicles* (Paul Stewart and Chris Riddell, Corgi)

Historical: *Tom's War* (Robert Leeson, Puffin), *Power and Stone* (Alice Leader, Puffin), *Goodnight Mister Tom* (Michelle Magorian, Puffin), *The Saga of Erik the Viking* (Michael Foreman, Puffin), *Carrie's War* (Nina Bawden, Puffin), *Out of the Shadow* (Margaret Nash, A and C Black)

Useful books of poems

The Works (chosen by Paul Cookson, Macmillan), *The Works 2* (chosen by Brian Moses and Pie Corbett, Macmillan), *I Like This Poem* (chosen by Kaye Webb, Puffin), *The Hutchinson Treasury of Children's Poetry* (edited by Alison Sage, Hutchinson), *The Kingfisher Book of Children's Poetry* (selected by Michael Rosen, Kingfisher), *The Puffin Book of Twentieth-Century Children's Verse* (edited by Brian Patten, Puffin), *The Poetry Book: Poems for Children* (chosen by Fiona Waters, Dolphin), *Read Me: A Poem A Day For The National Year of Reading* and *Read Me 2: A Poem for Every Day of the Year* (chosen by Gaby Morgan, Macmillan), *Classic Poems to Read Aloud* (selected by James Berry, Kingfisher), *The Oxford Treasury of Classic Poems*, OUP

Useful websites

Narrative

Reviews by 10–15 year-olds http://www.cool-reads.co.uk/
http://www.literacytrust.org.uk/links/webchild.html
http://www.kingston.gov.uk/browse/leisure/libraries/childrens_library_service/dual_language.htm (dual-language books)
Selected fiction and non-fiction books and book boxes:
http://www.badger-publishing.co.uk/
http://www.madeleinelindley.com/aboutus.aspx
The Piano by Aidan Gibbons: for links using IWB software see the Primary Strategy.

The following work without IWB software:
http://www.gutenberg.org/dirs/etext99/rlwyc10.txt
http://video.google.com/videoplay?docid=5422822544003533526
http://www.gutenberg.org/wiki/Main_Page
http://www.bartleby.com/ (classic texts online)

Non-fiction

Biography and autobiography

Journalistic writing

http://www.bbc.co.uk/radio4/gfi/?focuswin (Radio 4 children's magazine programme – listen to previous or current programmes online)

http://www.newsademic.com/ (children's newspapers)
http://news.bbc.co.uk/cbbcnews/hi/uk/default.stm (a news site for children)

Poetry

http://www.bbc.co.uk/radio4/gfi/?focuswin (Radio 4 children's magazine programme – listen to previous or current programmes online)
http://www.newsademic.com/ (children's newspapers)
http://news.bbc.co.uk/cbbcnews/hi/uk/default.stm (a news site for children)

The following notes expand upon those which are provided at the bottom of most activity pages. They give ideas and suggestions for making the most of the activity sheet, including suggestions for the whole-class introduction, the plenary session or for follow-up work using an adapted version of the activity sheet. To help teachers to select appropriate learning experiences for their pupils, the activities are grouped into sections within each book but the pages need not be presented in the order in which they appear, unless otherwise stated.

The book is split into three main sections: Narrative, Non-fiction and Poetry. These are subdivided to match the Planning Units of the Primary Framework for Literacy.

Narrative

Fiction genres

> The activities in this section focus on adventure and mystery stories and stories set in imaginary worlds. It is assumed that the children will first have read and discussed stories from different genres and be able to identify their key characteristics. Here they have opportunities to use what they have learned to help them to write their own stories in specific genres.

Adventure story recipe (page 13) helps the children to use a narrative technique to engage a reader – in this case, drawing the reader into a story via a photograph and an unexpected incident that starts the adventure. Prompts on the page remind the children of some of the key characteristics of adventure stories so that they will use them in their own writing. The children should first have read some adventure stories and identified the characteristics of the genre: an incident that sparks off the adventure, fast action, build-ups of excitement and tension, discoveries or surprises. These could be listed in display form. Ask them to explain how the author of a book they have read draws readers into the story and ask them to identify the incident that starts the adventure. Remind them also of their previous learning about story structure: opening → something happens → problem → resolution → ending. Encourage them to add other ingredients of their own to the 'recipe': for example, animals; unusual, special or magic objects; letters; signs or notices and also setbacks (for the main character), strokes of luck, surprises. The following activity (Adventure story starter) helps them to develop the story.

Adventure story starter (page 14) helps the children to use a narrative technique to engage and entertain the reader, using paragraphs to achieve pace. You could ask them to bring in photographs of elderly people from when they were in their schooldays – perhaps of their own grandparents – and rewrite the opening accordingly. Encourage them to include details from the photographs.

Adventure writer (page 15) helps the children to use a narrative technique to engage and entertain the reader, using paragraphs to achieve pace. They learn to plan, draft and write an engaging story in a specific genre and select words and language, drawing on their knowledge of literary features. You could first read the passage aloud (or ask one of the children to do this) and ask them if they think it sounds exciting. Ask them what could be done to make it more interesting and exciting.

Imaginary world: 1 and **2** (pages 16–17) help the children to plan, draft and write a mystery story. **Imaginary world: 1** provides an idea for an imaginary setting that the children can develop in their own ways. They could draw and annotate their ideas for the imaginary world inside the mountain. Once they have created their imaginary worlds, encourage them to question one another about them, to help them to refine these ideas. This could be presented as a 'hot-seating' activity. They can then introduce the imaginary world and its inhabitants in the opening of a story and introduce the main character. You could reread other stories set in imaginary worlds and focus on how much the author tells the reader about the place at the start and how other details emerge as the story progresses, as the reader needs to know about them. The children can then continue the story, introducing an incident that sets off a train of events and a problem for the main character to solve.

Children could expand the ideas in **Imaginary world: 2**, or use the sheet as a model for how they might begin/shape their own story, using their own notes from page 16.

Tense time (page 18) helps the children to use language to create the effect of tension. They should first have read mystery or adventure stories in which there are build-ups of tension at different points. Encourage them to write notes about each scene and then to use a thesaurus to help them to find the words that best build up an atmosphere of tension. Remind them of what they have learned about the connotations of words, about dialogue and monologue and varying the lengths of sentences.

Mystery starters (page 19) helps the children to use narrative techniques to engage and entertain the reader and to create tension and mystery. Ask them to make notes about what they know, from the starter provided, about the story so far, the setting and the characters, what mystery the story has to solve. They could talk to a partner about the mystery and use techniques they have learned from their reading: flashback, letters, newspaper reports and so on, to help them to tell the story.

Extending narrative

In these activities the children use what they have learned from non-linear, quest-type adventure stories and computer software they have read or played with to capture their reader's interest. They use what they have learned about organisational features to plan their own stories, using language to add interest.

Quest choices (page 20) focuses on the structure of a non-linear quest story. Ask the children to consider the choices the character can make and then the choices they lead to, and so on, focusing on the consequences of the choices. Remind them of what they have learned about the features and structure of a quest and the ways in which a character's choices affect events and the final outcome of a story. The children write two scenarios that might arise from taking a particular option, for example Internet search: 1) find out 'altifund' is a place, decide whether to go there or tell someone, 2) find out 'altifund' is an ancient treasure, decide whether to seek it out or tell someone.

The Casket of Attar: 1 and **2** (pages 21–22) focus on the setting and structure of a quest. It incorporates the features of quest stories that the children will have identified in quest stories they have read and quest games they have played. They could talk to a partner about what might happen in different parts of the castle: for example, challenges the characters might face there or objects they find that help them to overcome the challenges and to complete the quest. The story starter (page 22) provides a scenario and hints about ways of writing their story in a way that will engage the reader's interest. For ideas about castles, the award-winning *Castle Diary* by Richard Platt and Chris Riddell is sure to inspire the children.

Quest story recipe (page 23) helps the children to plan a quest story. Before they begin it is useful to consider the quest-type adventures they have read and to discuss the categories the quests fall into: revenge, righting a wrong, preventing evil or finding an object or person. Remind them that a series of challenges helps to build up tension and excitement. Important objects could include magic or protective clothing, gadgets and so on, that will help the characters to overcome evil or opposition. There is also an opportunity in the extension activity to develop skills in writing story endings that do not 'tail off'. You could discuss whether the main character should always achieve the quest. Would it be a good story if the character failed to do this?

Authors and texts

> This section develops the children's use of reading journals by encouraging them to give their journal a sharper focus: how the author introduces characters, settings and events. They also explore the stories through drama and mime.

Exploring a character: a letter (page 24) helps the children to explore a character in a story. It is based on the Whitbread Children's Book of the Year prize-winning novel *Skellig* by David Almond (see also *Developing Literacy Understanding and Responding to Texts* Ages 10–11). Begin by asking the children how the main character, Michael, feels at the start of the story and about all the events and issues that are causing these feelings. This is also an opportunity to develop letter-writing skills, including the consideration of language register (the level of formality and how personal/impersonal the language should be). Point out the fairly formal language style of the beginning of the letter and remind the children that this is because it is written to a grown-up whom Michael does not know.

Blogs (page 25) is about exploring two characters in the same story and offers an opportunity for the children to write in role. It could be based on any novel the children have been reading. You could begin the lesson by asking the children about blogs that they know or read regularly. Ask them if they would use the same kind of language as in writing a letter (as on page 24) and, if not, why not – and how it would differ. Draw out that a blog is very informal and parts can be written in note form (i.e. not in complete sentences, and using short forms of words, including 'blog jargon').

Text it (page 26) helps the children to explore relationships between characters. They could work in pairs, enacting the roles of the two characters and could even send one another text messages using mobile phones. It is useful to compare the kind of language used in text messages with that used in letters (see page 24) and blogs (see page 25). Teachers could demonstrate (on a whiteboard perhaps) some examples of text abbreviations.

Short story with flashbacks

> This section develops skills in the use of flashbacks in writing a story and on film. It also builds on the children's ability to explore characters (see the previous section, Authors and texts).

The grandson's tale: 1, 2 and **3** (pages 27–29) focus on the use of narrative techniques by developing the children's skills in

using flashbacks as they write about the life of the pianist from *The Piano* by Aidan Gibbons from the point of view of the pianist's grandson, told through incidents the grandson remembers from his own time spent with his grandfather. Their story should open in the present, perhaps during a visit to the grandparents, a family gathering or a party or a day out. The flashbacks could be to earlier but similar events. Page 28 helps the children to focus on specific objects, words or sounds that trigger the flashbacks. The pianist's playing throughout the film provides the link for all the events. The children need to think of an activity for the grandson to use in the same way: for example, heading or dribbling a football, swinging (on a swing), skipping. The children could, in fact, move straight from sheet 1 to sheet 3.

Short story: 1, 2 and **3** (pages 30–32) help the children to use varied structures to shape and organise text coherently. They also develop skills in using different narrative techniques to engage and entertain readers and using words, images and sounds imaginatively as the make notes about Eppie from *Silas Marner* by George Eliot and tell her life story through the medium of a short film. They also develop skills in making notes and summarising. They should use what they have learned from watching films such as *The Piano* to help them to show how changes from past to present time can be suggested using different visual effects such as gestures, camera panning, editing effects and costume. They could work in groups to plan a film, using page 32 as a format on which they write a paragraph that describes the part of the story they want to tell and then describe the picture they think will tell this part of the story to the viewer. The outcome could be a still film comprising drawings of each scene; these could be shown with accompanying music. Or the children could enact each scene and make a video recording.

Non-fiction
Biography and autobiography

> These activities combine narrative with non-fiction. They help the children to use narrative techniques suitable for both biography and autobiography, including the appropriate use of the first or third person, writing facts in a way that indicates their opinion and their explicit and implicit points of view. They also use what they have learned about the structure and language styles of biographies and autobiographies and plan, research and write a biography and/or autobiography.

Finding out about Charles Dickens and **Author presentation** (pages 33–34) develops the children's understanding of biography, their ability to research and make notes. The children could choose an author whose books they enjoy or this could be started as a piece of collaborative writing for a group or class, based on the life and work of an author they have been reading at school. Useful sources of information on Dickens include the covers and introductions of novels by Dickens, biographical dictionaries and websites such as BBC History (http://www.bbc.co.uk/history/historic_figures/dickens_charles.shtml), Spartacus Educational (http://www.spartacus.schoolnet.co.uk/PRdickens.htm), Charles Dickens' birthplace museum (http://www.charlesdickensbirthplace.co.uk/). These activities can be linked with work on authors and texts as the children explore the ways in which Charles Dickens' writing was affected by his own life.

Talking head (page 35) focuses on integrating words and images imaginatively for a purpose. Ask the children about the similarities and differences between biography and autobiography and tell them that they are going to write about the life of someone from history as if it were an autobiography (in the first person and from the point of view of that person). The children will need to research and make notes about heir chosen character and to use what they have learned to help them to write this from the subject's point of view. The activity presents an autobiography, in the first person. It provides an opportunity to include activities to develop speaking and listening skills as the children record their scripts for use in a class museum. They could play these in conjunction with an image of the character's head on screen, thus developing   ICT skills.

A dog's life (page 36) develops skills in selecting words and language drawing on knowledge of literary features. To help the children to imagine the story from the dog's point of view, they could read passages from *Call of the Wild* or *White Fang*, both by Jack London, which are written from the point of view of wolves and dogs (see http://www.gutenberg.org/dirs/etext95/callw10.txt and http://www.gutenberg.org/files/910/910-h/910-h.htm for online text). Remind the children that an autobiography is not simply a biography written in the first person, but that it presents events and situations from the subject's point of view, which includes their knowledge, thoughts and feelings.

Same life – different views: 1 and **2** (pages 37–38) develop skills in selecting words and language. It explores the ways in which a biographical account can be written in order to present different impressions of the same person. The children explore ways of writing the same facts in two different ways in order to present two different views.

Journalistic writing

This section is about writing news reports, using what has been learned about the language style of journalistic writing, and evaluating them. Discuss this type of reporting: its function and pleasures, why people write it, why people read it. You could link this work with citizenship (Citizenship scheme of work Unit 12 *'In the media – what's the news?'*) or geography (Geography scheme of work Unit 16 *'What's in the news?'*) and draw on it to develop speaking and listening skills (using the techniques of dialogic talk to explore ideas, topics or issues, considering examples of conflicts and resolution, exploring the language used). These activities could be used to develop literacy skills from work in citizenship ('*In the media – what's the news?'*)

Notes to news (page 39) is about using paragraphs to achieve pace and emphasis and using narrative techniques to engage the reader. First read news reports from a local newspaper with the children and draw their attention to the important features: a headline that tells readers what the article is about and attracts their attention; an introduction that gives a little more information and holds their interest so that they want to read on; a story, written briefly, that answers the questions *What?*, *Where?*, *Who?*, *When?*, *How?* and, sometimes, *Why?*, quotations from the people involved and a very brief summary or comment at the end. The page provides a format to help the children to structure their news item and to ensure that it answers the important questions *Who? What? Where? When?* and *How?* (In this example, the question *Why?* is not featured, since the children are writing a recount.)

Radio news (page 40) provides an opportunity for the children to set their own challenges to extend achievement and experience in writing as they use what they have learned about content of news reports (that they should answer the 'five W' questions: *Who? What? Where? When?* and *Why?* and might also answer the question *How?*) They also use what they have learned from their reading to help them to write for a specific audience (younger children). This activity can be presented as a group activity where groups of about four are given a topic to write about or choose one that is relevant to the school. Once they have written the story, ask them to check that it meets all the criteria they have identified and, if necessary, to edit it to ensure that it does. Record the report if possible – for example, as a podcast. Children should have the chance to hear recordings of radio news etc., as some of them may not be familiar with its features. Explain to the children that, like a newspaper, a radio news programme introduces stories through a series of headlines before telling the stories. There might be one or more presenters reading the general news, weather, business and other types of news; there might be interviews with other reporters, experts or members of the public. News items are strictly timed; this limits the amount of information that can be given, whereas with newspapers, readers can spend as long as they need to read each story.

News evaluation (page 41) helps the children to set their own challenges to extend achievement and experience in writing and then to evaluate their achievements against criteria they have identified from their reading (or their listening or viewing) of radio or television reports. They should justify their responses using evidence from their work.

News editor (page 42) focuses on the language used in a newspaper report, developing skills in using narrative techniques to engage the reader and select words and language, drawing on their knowledge of formal writing. The children are also required to improve the structure of sentences, for example:

> Heavy snow led to numerous postponements of Pentham Under-11 Football League matches this weekend. Snow 30 centimetres deep covered Gateway's and Cargill's pitches.
>
> In the only match one of the twelve to be played – Rodley v Minedale Bears – the away team narrowly avoided relegation, beating Rodley by one goal to nil. The goal was booted in from about two metres by Andy Cross from a superb cross from the right wing.
>
> Three fine second-half saves from goalkeeper Sally Holder kept out cracking shots from Ali Khan, James Boote and Anna Header.
>
> "It was a close game with great shots from both teams, but Sally saved the game for us," said Jenny Tacklit, Rodley's captain.

The proofreading symbols should be written in the appropriate places in the text and in the margins, with any inserted text written in the margin or, if room, above the existing text that is deleted.

Sports reporter (page 43) is about using a structure to shape and organise text coherently. It also focuses on the language used in a newspaper report, developing skills in using narrative techniques to engage the reader and select words and language, drawing on their knowledge of formal writing. The limited space on the page encourages the children to write succinctly. It might help if they first write a draft and then edit it to fit the space. If the CD is used the children could be given a word count for their report and edit it on screen to meet the required number of words, within a margin of about 15 to 20 words. When introducing the activity, focus awareness on the level of information needed by the reader. Ensure that children do not lose sight of what the reader knows or needs to know, and to pack together too much of the relevant terminology, etc.

Planners' point of view (page 44) builds the children's appreciation of the power and potential of communication media in presenting points of view so that they develop an understanding of how to establish and maintain a balanced viewpoint in non-narrative writing. In rewriting the report from the planners' point of view they should select words and phrases that emphasise positive effects of the wind farm on the environment and the improvement it offers to the local area (replacing derelict buildings – 'an eyesore' – and thus improving the view for residents). They should also emphasise the 'high-tech' benefits and the cleanliness and sustainability of wind power. Encourage them to try out different words and phrases in the text and to compare their effects. A biased version of the text is likely to include more extremes of language and emphasis, and rhetorical effects.

Argument

These activities support work on non-narrative writing in which balanced viewpoints are established and maintained. The children use key language features they have learned about in their reading of, or listening to, arguments. They also explore the use of structures of arguments in print or other media. There are opportunities for developing speaking and listening skills (using a range of oral techniques to present a persuasive argument; listening to analyse how speakers present points effectively through use of language and (where appropriate) gesture; making notes when listening for a sustained period and discussing how note-taking varies depending on context and purpose).

Cooking for all and **To cook or not to cook** (pages 45–46) are about carrying out research in order to present an effective argument, maintaining a particular viewpoint, using paragraphs to structure a text coherently and using language features, such as connective and rhetorical questions to present a convincing argument through formal language. The children write a one-sided argument which can later be compared with a more balanced argument. This could be linked with work in citizenship on Taking part (developing skills of communication and participation) and Choices. The children could present their views on compulsory cookery lessons for all in a class debate. During the plenary session, ask them if they changed their views after listening to the arguments of others and, if so, which arguments were the most convincing. Useful sources of information include:

http://www.bbc.co.uk/food/food_matters/schoolcookery.shtml
http://news.bbc.co.uk/1/hi/education/7202124.stm
http://publications.teachernet.gov.uk/eOrderingDownload/Cookery-guide-2006.pdf.

Sum it up (page 47) provides a format to help the children to note down the key points on different sides of an argument and to draw a conclusion based on these points. It also supports the development of speaking and listening skills: making notes for a sustained period and participating in a whole-class debate. The issue under discussion could arise from another area of the curriculum: for example, geography (investigating coasts, including the effects of industry and tourism) or citizenship (animal rights or environmental issues). See also the questions suggested for discussion for page 48.

Question it (page 48) focuses on non-narrative writing that establishes balance. The children read a biased text and are encouraged to consider other points of view and express these through questions. Encourage them to think of the possible advantages of 'mini-planes' that people could use like cars – also how their use might be managed safely. This could also form the basis of a class debate (with children preparing speeches to convince the others), culminating with a vote (see page 49).

Class debate (page 49) helps the children to question a one-sided argument. During the plenary session it is useful to draw out how the ideas from the questions could be used to make the argument more balanced. The issue debated could be the same that the children have already researched for earlier activities or they could be allowed time to research a new issue. This format could also be used as children listen to or watch a radio/television debate (e.g. on a programme such as *Any Questions* or *Question time*).

Formal/impersonal writing

This section is about the use of official language in formal situations and identifying and using the characteristic features of this language style: such as headings, precise vocabulary, and avoidance of slang, dialect words and contracted words.

Make it formal (page 50) helps the children to select words and language, drawing on their knowledge of formal and informal writing or to recognise occasions when an informal style of language is suitable and when a more formal style is appropriate. You could first invite a volunteer to give another child (acting as a newcomer) a tour of the classroom in the way he or she would normally speak to others of the same age. Then invite him or her to repeat this for an 'adult visitor' (if possible, arrange for an adult to come in to enact this). Examples of the

ways in which they could change the language to make it more formal and impersonal include: *Many items are donated by neighbours: for example, this old gate which one gentleman was very fond of and which he painted his favourite colour, blue, because he was given a large quantity of blue paint.* The change from speech to writing requires more specificity – pronouns that suggest the audience is present (*on that little wall*, *that patch*) need to be adjusted. Also discuss the fact that leaflets might vary in their formality, for example, a leaflet written for young visitors to the garden would probably be less formal than one written for adults.

Guide to Stadium School: 1 and **2** (pages 51–52) develops skills in planning a presentation that combines writing with different modes of communication and using ICT to create an interactive text. Pick a fictional school. This activity helps the children to plan and write a non-fiction presentation of information, using paragraphs to structure a text. They should regard the notes in each box on page 51 as notes for a separate section of the interactive guide. Use these pages for planning. The children will need to use a computer for writing their interactive guide. To insert a hyperlink, click Insert on the menu bar, and then click Hyperlink. The link could open a document, page of text, photograph, diagram, map, audio or video file. Link this with work in ICT (Multimedia presentation). Children could evaluate and try out each other's work, and provide feedback.

Formal notice (page 53) is about the vocabulary of formal language. The children select words and language drawing on their knowledge of formal writing. If possible, provide a thesaurus that gives separate informal and formal alternatives for words. It would be good to recap the reasons why this kind of notice might need to be formal in style, e.g. the serious aspect of 'conditions' in these circumstances, where large groups of people are involved.

Voice-over (page 54) develops skills in planning a presentation that combines writing with different modes of communication and using ICT to create an interactive text. The children should have the opportunity to take photographs, make maps, make video and audio recordings and draw sketches and diagrams as well as locating and reading information about the place. You could combine this with work in citizenship (respect for property; developing our school grounds) and geography (connecting ourselves to the world). As a class you could choose a particular venue for the virtual tour, e.g. an adventure holiday centre.

Poetry

The power of imagery

Here the children explore ways of using personification in poems to communicate powerful images to the reader or listener and write poems that begin to use personification effectively.

Getting personal (page 55) focuses on playing with language in order to communicate a powerful image of a thunderstorm, imagining the thunderstorm as a person – probably an angry person. They should imagine how this person might think, speak and move.

Traffic personified (page 56) supports the children in writing a poem that begins to use personification effectively. They could imagine the traffic flowing through someone's arteries and veins and the throb of the engines as a heartbeat.

Images of people (page 57) helps the children to develop ideas for poems that attempt to see things in a new light using amusing images as they develop ideas for presenting images of people inspired by fruit. This could be based on famous people or television and film characters.

De-personified (page 58) helps the children to create images of people using images of non-human objects or scenes. Use the examples to demonstrate how the sounds of words can contribute to the images: for example, the soft effect *ff* sounds in *A puff of a girl* and *A puff of air* and the mysterious effect of the long vowel sounds in *A deep pool*, *seemed*, *time* and *brewing wise words* – enhanced by the alliteration of *w*. The children could also use drama to explore the way in which their descriptions personify each person.

Wacky poem and **Wacky poem cards** (pages 59–60) encourage the children to create surreal, surprising and amusing imagery, drawing on what they learn from *Out of Sight* by Roger McGough. They model their poems on the structure of Roger McGough's poem but think up a different surreal and amusing image for the ending. The cards suggest some ideas to get them started.

Finding a voice

This section provides activities to help the children to express their thoughts and feelings about issues, exploring imagery, language and the structure of poems to communicate with readers and listeners.

Abandoned: 1 and **2** (pages 61–62) provide a format to help the children to research and make notes about an issue which forms the subject of a poem and to express feelings about the issue through revealing the dog's thoughts in speech bubbles. The speech bubbles can then be used as the basis of a monologue, as if spoken by the abandoned dog, which addresses the reader directly.
Useful websites include www.rspca.org.uk, www.pdas.org.uk, www.dogpages.org.uk/, www.dogstrust.org.uk/.

The last passenger pigeon and **Passenger pigeon rap** (pages 63–64) invite the children to respond to the story of the extinction of the passenger pigeon and then explore language to express their feelings through poetry. Encourage them to use what they have learned about imagery in the previous section (The power of imagery) to express these feelings. Different groups, writing raps to express different opinions and feelings, could present their raps as arguments to persuade others. This could be linked with non-fiction writing of arguments.

Using the CD-ROM

The CD-ROM included with this book contains an easy-to-use software program that allows you to print out pages from the book, to view them (e.g. on an interactive whiteboard) or to customise the activities to suit the needs of your pupils.

Getting started

It's easy to run the software. Simply insert the CD-ROM into your CD drive and the disk should autorun and launch the interface in your web browser.

If the disk does not autorun, open 'My Computer' and select the CD drive, then open the file 'start.html'.

Please note: this CD-ROM is designed for use on a PC. It will also run on most Apple Macintosh computers in Safari however, due to the differences between Mac and PC fonts, you may experience some unavoidable variations in the typography and page layouts of the activity sheets.

The Menu screen

Four options are available to you from the main menu screen.

The first option takes you to the Activity Sheets screen, where you can choose an activity sheet to edit or print out using Microsoft Word.

(If you do not have the Microsoft Office suite, you might like to consider using OpenOffice instead. This is a multi-platform and multi-lingual office suite, and an 'open-source' project. It is compatible with all other major office suites, and the product is free to download, use and distribute. The homepage for OpenOffice on the Internet is: www.openoffice.org.)

The second option on the main menu screen opens a PDF file of the entire book using Adobe Reader (see below). This format is ideal for printing out copies of the activity sheets or for displaying them, for example on an interactive whiteboard.

The third option allows you to choose a page to edit from a text-only list of the activity sheets, as an alternative to the graphical interface on the Activity Sheets screen.

Adobe Reader is free to download and to use. If it is not already installed on your computer, the fourth link takes you to the download page on the Adobe website.

You can also navigate directly to any of the three screens at any time by using the tabs at the top.

The Activity Sheets screen

This screen shows thumbnails of all the activity sheets in the book. Rolling the mouse over a thumbnail highlights the page number and also brings up a preview image of the page.

Click on the thumbnail to open a version of the page in Microsoft Word (or an equivalent software program, see above.) The full range of editing tools are available to you here to customise the page to suit the needs of your particular pupils. You can print out copies of the page or save a copy of your edited version onto your computer.

The Index screen

This is a text-only version of the Activity Sheets screen described above. Choose an activity sheet and click on the 'download' link to open a version of the page in Microsoft Word to edit or print out.

Technical support

If you have any questions regarding the *100% New Developing Literacy* or *Developing Mathematics* software, please email us at the address below. We will get back to you as quickly as possible.

educationalsales@acblack.com

Adventure story recipe

- **Plan an adventure story using the ingredients in the recipe.**

> Add other ingredients of your own.

an old school photograph from (when?) ☐

_____

a silver pointer ☐

main character (present-day) who looks at the photograph ☐

_____

other present-day characters ☐

_____

_____

a key character from the photograph ☐

_____

other characters from the photograph ☐

_____

a character who causes problems ☐

_____

Other ingredients

_____

_____

_____

an exciting incident ☐
(when the main character uses the silver pointer to point to someone in the photograph)

_____

_____

action: moving through different settings ☐

_____

_____

build-ups ☐
(incidents that keep up the excitement)

_____

_____

discoveries ☐
(what the main character learns)

_____

_____

Other ingredients

_____

_____

_____

NOW TRY THIS!

- **Write notes about what happens in your story.**

Teachers' note Discuss an adventure story in relation to stories the children know before they start planning their own story. Children tick the elements they want to include and make notes about them.

Adventure story starter

- **Complete the opening paragraphs of this adventure story about an old school photograph.**

Can you use some ideas from your story recipe?

In some ways it was like Mark's own school photo: two rows of ten- and eleven-year-olds smiling, grinning mischievously or gazing sullenly at the camera. It was in black, white and shades of grey and a little frayed at the edges. The boys wore short grey trousers and the girls wore grey skirts with a pinafore top attached. The boys wore grey socks that came up to their knees but the girls wore white ankle socks. All the children were dressed in white shirts and striped ties.

Mark looked at his grandmother – smiling, cross-legged in the front row, showing a plaster on one knee. Her fair hair was tied with ribbons. She had died before he was born.

A long time ago he had found an old silver pointer in a drawer in the kitchen. His father said it had been there when his grandfather gave him the old pine dresser. Mark had put the pointer into the box with the photograph album. He picked it up and rested the tip on the smiling face of his grandmother. Then he saw a smudge.

"Oh, no!" he thought.
"I've scratched the photo."

He looked again. The girl with the hair ribbons was now standing. She looked up at him.

_____

_____

_____

_____

_____

_____

_____

_____

_____

_____

NOW TRY THIS!

- **Reread what you wrote.**
- **See if you can make the language more exciting.**

Use dialogue, powerful verbs, and interesting adjectives and adverbs. Use sentences of different lengths.

Teachers' note The children should first have completed page 13. You could read the passage with them and ask them for suggestions about what might happen next. What might Mark do? Where might he go? What might the girl in the photograph (his grandmother as a child) do and say? Is he imagining it?

100% New Developing Literacy
Creating and Shaping Texts:
Ages 10–11
© A & C BLACK

Adventure writer

- **Improve these paragraphs from an adventure story.**
  Make it more exciting:
  Change the words in bold type.
  Use more powerful verbs.
  Add expressive nouns, adjectives or adverbs.
  Write the missing parts.

Serena **cried** with pain and fear. Tears **ran** down her face. The others had **gone**. Her **cries** filled the air. She had to find the way through the woods. But which way? They had been **going** east but a mist hid the sun. Why were the woods so **quiet**? Where were the birds and other animals? The mist thickened, then Serena smelled something that **scared** her. Smoke. That meant fire. Then she saw it.

_____

_____

> Describe what she saw.

Serena's lungs felt as if they would burst as she **ran**, hoping she was running away from the fire. She ran and ran. She heard the **sound** of the fire behind her,

_____

> Describe what she heard.

The burning air singed her denim jacket as she ran. "Faster!" she **said** to herself.

_____

_____

_____

_____

_____

_____

_____

_____

NOW TRY THIS!

- **Write the next paragraph.**

> Make it sound exciting.

Teachers' note Remind the children of what they have learned about choosing words that help to conjure up an image or communicate feelings, mood or atmosphere: for example, _cried_ (_called, screamed, sobbed, whimpered, wailed, yelled_). Ask them about the image each word creates and which they think is best here.

100% New Developing Literacy
Creating and Shaping Texts:
Ages 10–11
© A & C BLACK

Imaginary world: 1

- Complete the map of an imaginary world inside a mountain.
- Invent objects such as plants, materials, machines and technology.
- Make up names that describe them.

Include danger zones and secret places known only to very few inhabitants.

NOW TRY THIS!

- What might happen to start the story?
- Write notes about the first key event.

**100% New Developing Literacy
Creating and Shaping Texts:
Ages 10–11**
© A & C BLACK

Imaginary world: 2

- **Complete the opening paragraphs for a story set in an imaginary world inside a mountain.**
Introduce the main character and the setting.

Far, far down, inside the mountain is _____ , a dark mysterious land. Long tunnels and wide caverns are linked by thousands of tube-like passages through the rock. Down one chasm a vast torrent of water falls into a vast black pool deep within the mountain.

_____

_____

_____

_____

Give the land a name. Say more about it.

In this dark world live four known types of beings: the _____ , the _____ , the _____ and the _____ . It is thought that others have invaded and are living there in secret.

_____

_____

Name the beings who live there. Say what they look like, and describe their ways of life. Introduce the ideas of danger and conflict.

_____ sat on the _____ in the _____ of the _____ , looking at _____ .

_____

_____

_____

_____

Introduce and describe the main character and his or her home and family. Recount a typical day in their life. Use words that suggest fear and danger.

NOW TRY THIS!

- **Reread your paragraphs. Edit them. See if you can use more expressive adjectives, adverbs and verbs.**

Think about the effects of words.

Teachers' note The children should first have completed page 16. They could make annotated drawings of their imaginary characters, adding notes about their backgrounds, personal qualities, characteristics and what they are trying to do. Encourage them to introduce a conflict, which might arise from the conflicting aims of the characters.

**100% New Developing Literacy
Creating and Shaping Texts:
Ages 10–11**
© A & C BLACK

Tense time

- **Write paragraphs from the notes.**
- **Build up tension in each paragraph.**

Write in the past tense.

Notes	Paragraph
Alankar wakes in middle of night. Hears scraping noise above ceiling.	_____ _____ _____ _____ _____ _____ _____

Describe what the characters saw and heard.

Use powerful verbs for movements and sounds.

Ella follows two men into forest. They have stolen a v. important data pen.	_____ _____ _____ _____ _____ _____

Use expressive adjectives.

Write sentences of different lengths.

Message on Simon's mobile phone. Doesn't recognise voice giving him instructions.	_____ _____ _____ _____ _____ _____

Think about the effects of words.

Write the characters' thoughts using speech marks.

NOW TRY THIS!

- **Choose one of the paragraphs. Write the rest of the chapter.**

Teachers' note Discuss how authors of mystery or adventure stories create tension through the use of language: sentence structure and length, dialogue, monologue or a character's thoughts, and choice of words. Ask them to begin by imagining the first scene. What is Alankar doing? What are his thoughts?

100% New Developing Literacy
Creating and Shaping Texts:
Ages 10–11
© A & C BLACK

Mystery starters

Sirrillo knows that he does not belong to the family of Space Trolls he lives with. He came from another planet to Poseidon as a baby eleven years ago. 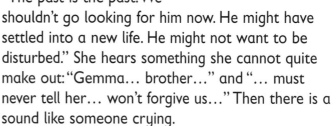 His adopted parents are kind to him and he loves them and his brothers, but he wants to find the family he came from. He arrived with only his shiny blue metal suit and helmet that no longer fit him. In a pocket was a small blue metal disc with a picture of a bird on it. The bird has huge wings and a hooked beak. It is unlike any birds on Poseidon. On the back is an inscription, but neither Sirrillo nor any of his family can read it.

Gemma overhears her mother and father talking about someone they call Paul. They seem sad that they do not know where he is, but Gemma's father says "The past is the past. We shouldn't go looking for him now. He might have settled into a new life. He might not want to be disturbed." She hears something she cannot quite make out: "Gemma… brother…" and "… must never tell her… won't forgive us…" Then there is a sound like someone crying.

Rashid finds an old wooden chest in the attic, locked with a big padlock. He is sure his uncle has the key. He has heard his uncle and aunt talking about an old chest that sounds just like this one, but they do not know where it is: "We'd be rich… If only I could find it… Maybe it was left in India…"

Rashid's parents do not know where the chest is. Their house belonged to their parents – Rashid's grandparents. They moved there from India long ago. The family still use some of their furniture. They often find interesting pictures and letters at the backs of drawers and cupboards.

Astrid has been listening to her family's talk about the farm and land they used to own in Iceland. They moved to London when she was a baby but they  wanted her to know about her ancestors. She asks what happened to the family's lands. Her parents mutter something about it not being fair and "that layabout Knut" and "wasted". Astrid wants to know where the farm was. "Up north… beautiful moors… he'd never let any of us onto the land." She cannot find out why no-one in the family speaks to Knut and why they resent him having the farm.

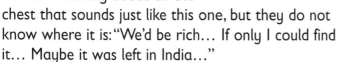

1932. Twelve-year-old Thomas enjoys going into the attic rooms in the big old house in Liverpool and just looking out over the city, watching. He also likes rummaging around in old boxes stored there. He comes across a box of photographs: a man of about 40, a family group, two young men, a wedding, four boys on a picnic. He realises that one person is in all the photographs, but at different ages. Thomas is sure he has never seen this man before in photographs that he has looked at with his mother – so often that he feels he knows everyone in them.

In the churchyard Sally hears a knocking – like someone knocking on a wooden door, then a voice coming from a grave: "Tell Jack to  get out of my house. It belongs to Nina. Look for my will under the kitchen floorboards." She is scared and wonders if someone has been buried alive and she should tell the police. The inscription is old and worn: P___R GR____ DIED 31 OC_____18__ AGED 39. 31st October – today's date but some time in the 1800s. She calls out "Who are you?" No answer. She listens – nothing – and wonders if she imagined it. She is sure she didn't. She wants to find out more.

Teachers' note Cut out the cards so that the children have one each: each group could work on the same card or they could be distributed at random or the children could choose one. They can make notes about the setting and character. This might involve some research, before planning a story in which the character solves the mystery.

100% New Developing Literacy Creating and Shaping Texts: Ages 10–11 © A & C BLACK

Quest choices

What could Caspar do next?

- Write other actions he could choose.
- Continue the flowchart.

I have to find the Earth Nerve centre before Omenblast does.

The word 'altifund' is important but I don't know why.

Caspar's options

Do an Internet search for 'altifund'.

Get into the Terra Quest building, where he first heard the word.

Visit his Uncle Hardgrim, whose expression changed when Caspar asked about 'altifund'.

NOW TRY THIS!

- Write a chapter about one of the choices Caspar makes.

What happens as a result of this choice?

Teachers' note Remind the children of quest stories they have read or quest games they have played and about how a character's choices affect what happens in the story or game. This page could be used for planning a quest game or story in which there is a choice of outcomes.

100% New Developing Literacy
Creating and Shaping Texts:
Ages 10–11
© A & C BLACK

The Casket of Attar: 1

The quest is to find the **Casket of Attar**, which is hidden in a secret chamber in the **Castle of Attar**.
No one knows what it contains.
The quest-seekers never know who else is also searching for it.
How can the quest-seekers find the secret chamber?

• Make notes about what they might find or what they can do in each part of the **Castle of Attar**. Write on the plan.

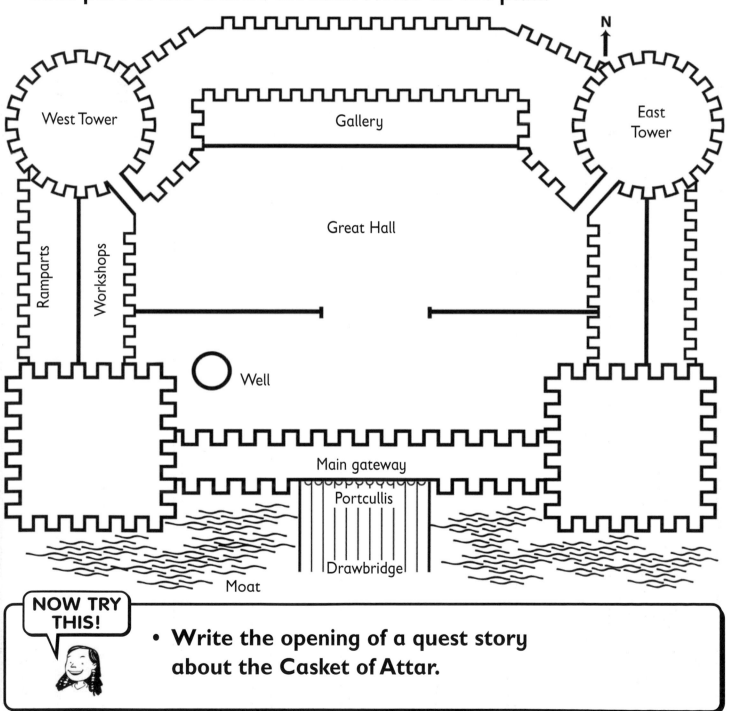

West Tower

Gallery

East Tower

N

Great Hall

Ramparts

Workshops

Well

Main gateway

Portcullis

Drawbridge

Moat

NOW TRY THIS!

• **Write the opening of a quest story about the Casket of Attar.**

Teachers' note Use this alongside page 22. The children annotate an enlarged copy of the plan or use the CD-ROM with their ideas about who is searching for the casket, how they get into the castle and what happens in different places. Ask them to think of challenges the characters face in each place and their struggles to survive them.

100% New Developing Literacy
Creating and Shaping Texts:
Ages 10–11
© A & C BLACK

The Casket of Attar: 2

- **Use the chapter notes to help you to write the opening of this chapter of the *Casket of Attar*.**

The story so far

The Casket of Attar was hidden in the Castle of Attar four hundred years ago. Sealgrey and Skyblu have reached the castle after a journey of a thousand miles. They know that others might also be working on the coded documents they discovered in the British Library in London – and might already have arrived on the island of Attar. They have to work quickly.

> **Notes**
>
> Seal & Sky picked up gold key on beach. Found long cave – followed tunnels. Way was barred by grille. Padlocked. Gold key fitted. Up stone staircase into West Tower. Saw old broom, bent shield & pike in corner. Up ladder to top of tower. Circular room. 3-headed monster in centre. Weapons would be useful. Should they go back for shield & pike?

> Describe the scene. Describe the key and say how and where they found it.

> Write the dialogue.

> Recount how they got into the castle.

> Use language that creates the atmosphere of the scene.

_____

_____

_____

_____

_____

_____

_____

_____

_____

NOW TRY THIS!

- **Reread the chapter opening.**
- **Find ways to make it more exciting.**

> Check for uninteresting verbs. Make them more powerful. Add adjectives and adverbs.

Teachers' note Use this alongside page 21. Ask the children to recount the scene in the notes and to think about the atmosphere they want to create as well as the details of the scene. They should include dialogue between Seal and Sky that expresses their feelings. Remind them of their previous work on expressive language: powerful verbs and so on.

100% New Developing Literacy
Creating and Shaping Texts:
Ages 10–11
© A & C BLACK

Quest story recipe

- **Write notes on the recipe to help you to plan a quest story.**

Ingredients

Main character(s)

Other characters

Important objects

The quest: for example, to find something, to find information, to put something right

Challenges the main character faces

Plan (chapters)

1 _____

_____

2 _____

_____

3 _____

_____

4 _____

_____

5 _____

_____

6 _____

_____

 **NOW TRY THIS!**

- **Write the ending of the story.**

Teachers' note The children could use this to help them to plan the story of the Casket of Attar or another quest story. Ask them to name and describe their main character and other key characters and to say what the quest is.

100% New Developing Literacy Creating and Shaping Texts: Ages 10–11 © A & C BLACK

Exploring a character: a letter

Michael, in *Skellig* by David Almond, is worried and unhappy.
- **Write a letter from Michael to a problem page in a magazine.**
- **Describe his worries and feelings.**

Add details from the story. Write the date and make up an address for Michael using information from the story. Make up a name for the problem-page adviser.

_____

_____

_____

_____

Dear _____
I hope you can give me some advice. We have just moved house _____

_____

_____

_____

_____

_____

_____

_____

_____

_____

Yours sincerely _____

NOW TRY THIS!

- **Write a reply to Michael from the problem-page adviser.**

Remember to lay out your letter correctly.

Teachers' note This is based on *Skellig* by David Almond (see Introduction page 7) but the details could be altered using the CD-ROM so that it could apply to any novel in which a character has worries or fears. The children could also read appropriate magazine problem pages and discuss the purpose of the letters and their responses.

24

100% New Developing Literacy
Creating and Shaping Texts:
Ages 10–11
© A & C BLACK

Blogs

- **Write blogs for two characters from a novel you know well.**
- **Show each character's thoughts and feelings about the same event or issue.**

Book title	Author

Event or issue

Write the facts.

Character's name	Character's name
Log	Log

Give each entry a date.

NOW TRY THIS!

- **Enact a dialogue in which you talk to one of these characters about the incident.**
- **Write the dialogue as a playscript.**

Work with a partner.

Teachers' note The children should first compare their style with that of other forms of communication, which will help them to explore any story characters, particularly those created by one author. It could be adapted for two characters from *different* stories. During the plenary session ask the children for evidence from the stories to justify what they wrote.

100% New Developing Literacy
Creating and Shaping Texts:
Ages 10–11
© A & C BLACK

Text it

- **Choose a key event or issue from a novel.**
- **Write a text message to a character in the book to comment or ask questions about the event or issue.**
- **Write the character's reply.**
- **Continue the text dialogue.**

Title _____

_____

Author _____

Character _____

Event or issue _____

_____

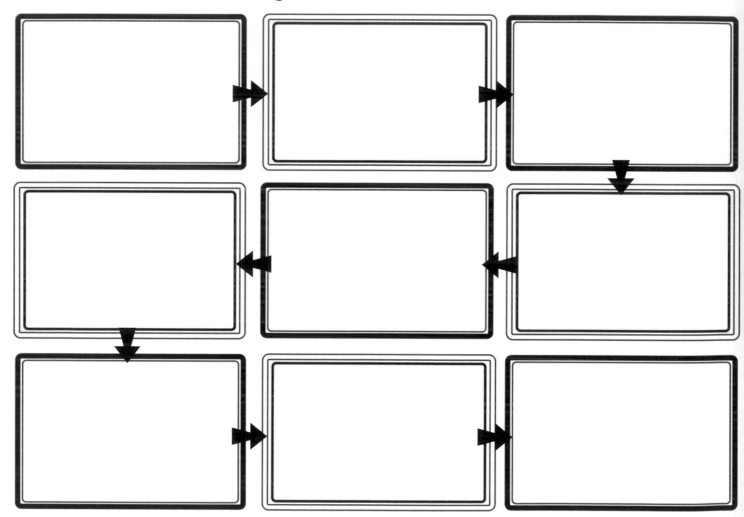

NOW TRY THIS!

- **Discuss your work with a partner who chose the same character.**
- **Make notes about what you have learned about the character.**

Hmmm... I wonder what they are really like?

Teachers' note You could select the story for this activity and let the children choose the characters for their text dialogue. Ask them to identify an important event in the story and to think about how it affected each character.

100% New Developing Literacy
Creating and Shaping Texts:
Ages 10–11
© A & C BLACK

The grandson's tale: 1

- **Watch the video *The Piano* by Aidan Gibbons.**
- **Plan a short story from the grandson's point of view.**
- **Begin at the present time.**
- **Use flashbacks.**

Write notes about events the grandson might remember about his grandfather from the past.

 Present

 Flashback

Present (Any changes since the first scene: actions, characters arriving/leaving, weather, time, light?)

 Flashback

Present (Any changes since the last 'present' scene?)

 Flashback

Present (Any changes since the last 'present' scene?)

Teachers' note The children should first have watched *The Piano* by Aidan Gibbons (see Introduction page 7). Ask the children to imagine some memories the pianist's grandson might have of time spent with his grandfather. Discuss any present-day events or objects that might trigger his memories. Continued on page 28.

100% New Developing Literacy
Creating and Shaping Texts:
Ages 10–11
© A & C BLACK

The grandson's tale: 2

- **Use your plan and notes to help you to write the opening and the first flashback of the grandson's story.**

Opening

> Think of an interesting opening sentence. For example, a question or statement to make the reader curious.

> Tell the story of why the family has gathered together. For example, a special occasion.

> Use dialogue.

_____

_____

_____

_____

_____

_____

_____

Flashback

> Link the flashback to the present time in the story. You could do this with an object, such as a photograph, a tree, a toy, music.

_____

_____

_____

_____

_____

_____

_____

_____

NOW TRY THIS!

- **Write the rest of the story.**
- **Think of different ways of moving between each flashback and the present.**

Teachers' note The children should first have completed page 27. Ask them for their ideas about the grandparents in the film, their grandson – and his parents, who do not appear. Encourage them to a family gathering and say who is there and what they talk about. This could lead to memories of past events.

100% New Developing Literacy
Creating and Shaping Texts:
Ages 10–11
© A & C BLACK

The grandson's tale: 3

• **Write a film script from your story. The film should last only two minutes.**

Choose the three key events.

Decide what to show on the screen.

Opening

What is the grandson doing all through the film?
This will link **all** the flashbacks.

Link

Think about facial expression, gesture, camera pan, change of colour, fading, images merging, change of costume.

Flashback 1

Flashback

Link

Flashback 2

Flashback

Link

Flashback 3

Flashback

Ending

Teachers' note The children should first have completed pages 27–28. They could watch the film *The Piano* again, focusing on the links between flashbacks and the present day. Remind them that their film, like the story they wrote, is from the grandson's point of view. His grandfather played the piano throughout the film: ask what the grandson could do throughout.

**100% New Developing Literacy
Creating and Shaping Texts:
Ages 10–11**
© A & C BLACK

1 This is the history of Silas Marner. The livelong day he sat at his loom, his eyes bent close down. At night he closed his shutters, and made fast his doors, and drew forth his gold. How the guineas shone as they came pouring out of the dark leather bags!

2 "I might tell the Squire how his handsome son was married to that nice young woman, Molly Farren, and was very unhappy because he couldn't live with his drunken wife, and I should slip into your place as comfortable as could be. You'll get the hundred pounds for me – I know you will," said Dunstan. "How can I get the money?" said Godfrey, quivering.

3 Silas got up from his knees, trembling, and looked round at the table. The table was bare. Then he turned and looked behind him – looked all round his dwelling, seeming to strain his brown eyes after some possible appearance of the bags where he had already sought them in vain. He could see every object in his cottage – and his gold was not there.

4 Molly now found herself in the snow-hidden ruggedness of the long lanes. She sank down against a straggling furze bush. She did not feel the cold, and did not heed whether the child would wake and cry for her. The little one she was carrying slumbered on as gently as if she had been rocked in a lace-trimmed cradle.

That week there was a funeral in Raveloe.

5 Silas Marner seated himself on his fireside chair, and was stooping to push his logs together, when, to his blurred vision, it seemed as if there were gold on the floor in front of the hearth. Gold – his own gold – brought back to him as mysteriously as it had been taken away! He felt his heart begin to beat violently. He leaned forward and stretched forth his hand but instead of the hard coin, his fingers encountered soft warm curls. Silas fell on his knees and bent his head low to examine the marvel: it was a sleeping child – a round, fair thing, with soft yellow rings all over its head.

6 "Why, you'd better leave the child here, then, Master Marner," said good-natured Mrs Kimble.

"No – no – I can't part with her, I can't let her go," said Silas abruptly. "She's come to me – I've a right to keep her."

7 "It's Dunstan – my brother Dunstan, that we lost sight of sixteen years ago. We've found him – found his body – his skeleton." The deep dread Godfrey's look had created in Nancy made her feel these words a relief. She sat in comparative calmness to hear what else he had to tell. He went on:

"The Stone-pit has gone dry; and there he has lain for sixteen years, wedged between two great stones. There's his watch and seals, and there's my gold-handled hunting-whip, with my name on: he took it away, without my knowing, the last time he was seen," said Godfrey. Presently he added: "Dunstan was the man that robbed Silas Marner."

Between eight and nine o'clock that evening, Eppie and Silas were seated alone in the cottage. On the table near them, lit by a candle, lay the gold recovered from the Stone-pit.

8 Godfrey had from the first specified Eppie, then about twelve years old, as a child suitable for them to adopt. It had never occurred to him that Silas would rather part with his life than with Eppie. Surely the weaver would be glad that such good fortune should happen to her.

Eppie held Silas's hand in hers, and grasped it firmly.

"Thank you, ma'am – thank you, sir, for your offers – they're very great, and far above my wish. For I should have no delight i'life any more if I was forced to go away from my father, and knew he was sitting at home a-thinking of me and feeling lone. We've been used to be happy together every day, and I can't think o' no happiness without him. And he says he'd nobody i'the world till I was sent to him, and he'd have nothing when I was gone. I'll cleave to him as long as he lives, and nobody shall ever come between him and me."

Adapted from *Silas Marner* by George Eliot

Teachers' note These passages are adapted from *Silas Marner* by George Eliot. You could also show the children the film. Tell them that the passages recount key moments in Silas Marner's life and ask them to write headlines to summarise them. Also ask them what they know about Eppie. See also page 31.

100% New Developing Literacy Creating and Shaping Texts: Ages 10–11 © A & C BLACK

Short story: 2

- **Plan Eppie's story using flashbacks.**
- **Begin and end with Eppie's wedding, which took place at the end of the story.**
- **Use arrows to link the flashbacks.**

Choose which parts of the story you need to use.

You could make up flashbacks such as Eppie's and other character's thoughts and memories, dialogue, newspaper cuttings, part of a Christian wedding or funeral service.

The sunshine fell more warmly than usual on the lilac tufts the morning that Eppie was married. One hand was on her husband's arm, and with the other she clasped the hand of her father Silas.

Raveloe Gazette

"You won't be giving me away, father," she had said before they went to church, "you'll only be taking Aaron to be a son to you."

Teachers' note The children should first have completed page 30. Ask them to note the key events in Eppie's life, using what they know from the passages on page 30 and this page (and the film, if they have seen it). Explain the use of letters, invitations and other documents to introduce a flashback in a story.

**100% New Developing Literacy
Creating and Shaping Texts:
Ages 4–5**
© A & C BLACK

31

Short story: 3

Write each paragraph as briefly as you tell the story.

Think about telling the story and showing the characters' feelings.

- **Underline the key moments.**
- **Make notes about how to show them in a 2½ minute film.**

Paragraph	Film
1 Silas Marner, the weaver, worked all day. At night he closed the shutters and locked up, then gazed at his gold.	
2	
3	
4	
5	
6	
7	
8	

Teachers' note The children need a copy of page 30 for reference. Ask them to compare the example paragraph with the original from the story. They should notice that only the key actions are recorded in the summary, without details of the scene. Ask them to describe how they imagine the scene and how they would capture it on film.

100% New Developing Literacy
Creating and Shaping Texts:
Ages 4–5
© A & C BLACK

Finding out about Charles Dickens

- **Find out some key facts about Charles Dickens.**
- **Make notes about them in the notebook.**
- **Use the facts to help you to answer the questions.**

Date and place of birth	Family
Key events in his childhood	Marriage and children
Work	Date, place and cause of death

 Why do you think Dickens wrote about children with family members in prison?

_____

_____

_____

 Why did poor children feature in many of Dickens' novels?

_____

_____

_____

 Why do you think debt was a theme of many of Dickens' novels?

_____

_____

_____

NOW TRY THIS!

- **What else would you like to know about how Dickens' life affected his writing?**
- **Write a question and find out the answer.**

Teachers' note Ask the children to suggest important details they need to know in order to write a biography and discuss the best sources in which to find the information. Tell them that this page helps them to organise research for a biography of Charles Dickens. Useful sources of information are listed in the Introduction on pages 7–8.

100% New Developing Literacy
Creating and Shaping Texts:
Ages 10–11
© A & C BLACK

Author presentation

- **Find out about the life of an author you like.**
- **Plan a talk about the author.**

Read biographical notes on book covers.

Check the author's website.

Find out when and where the author was born and grew up, and where he or she lives.

Introduction

The author I am going to talk about is _____

He/She lives/lived _____

Examples of his/her books are _____

_____

_____

Give evidence from the books, from biographical notes and the author's website.

Details

The genre _____

_____

He/She might have chosen this genre because _____

_____

The settings _____

_____

I think he/she chooses these settings because _____

_____

The theme(s) that most interest him/her is/are _____

_____

This might be because _____

_____

You could invite questions or make a comment.

Summary

_____

_____

NOW TRY THIS!

- **Find the answers to questions which others in your class have asked you.**
- **Write and display the questions and answers.**

Teachers' note Encourage the children to find out about incidents in the author's life and about his or her interests or concerns and to make links between these and the subjects, themes and characters in the books. Children could prepare one or two appropriate visual aids (images or objects) to enhance their presentation.

**100% New Developing Literacy
Creating and Shaping Texts:
Ages 10–11**
© A & C BLACK

Talking head

- **Find out about the life of a person from history.**
- **Prepare a 'talking head' hologram for a museum.**

I was born _____

_____

_____

My childhood _____

_____

_____

_____

My parents _____

_____

_____

_____

_____

Glue a picture of the person here.

When I grew up _____

_____

_____

_____

_____

The most important things
I have done _____

_____

_____

_____

_____

_____

_____

_____

_____

_____

_____

_____

_____

_____

_____

_____

_____

_____

_____

_____

NOW TRY THIS!

- **Record your talking head presentation as if you are the person.**
- **Play it back and make a note of anything you can improve.**

Did you change the pace, volume and tone of voice?

Teachers' note They are going to write about the life of someone from history as if it were an autobiography (in the first person and from the point of view of that person). Page 33 could be adapted to help them to record their research. The children's recordings could be saved on a computer for use in a class museum.

**100% New Developing Literacy
Creating and Shaping Texts:
Ages 10–11**
© A & C BLACK

A dog's life

- **Write about these scenes from the point of view of the dog.**

Think about what he saw, heard and felt – and what he thought.

Sarah picked him out immediately. "That one," she said, hardly looking at the others. Her father wasn't sure. "The others look better, with their long black and white hair," he said. But her mother liked the little tricolour collie, too. He was jumping up at the wire fence, gazing at them, tongue flapping, panting and wagging his tail.		_____
"No!" yelled Dad. "Bad dog!" He clapped his hands angrily at Tweed (that was the name they had given him) and grabbed his slipper – now with a large hole in the toe. Tweed crept under the table, as Dad complained bitterly about the three pairs of shoes, four gloves, a scarf and now a slipper that the "little so-and-so" had chewed.		_____
"Sit, Tweed," said Sarah firmly, holding a dog biscuit just too high for the puppy to reach. "No!" she said as he jumped to reach it. She tried again. This time she pushed his rump down gently. He lay down and wagged his tail. Sarah tried again. This time she held the biscuit above his nose as she gently pushed him into a sitting position. "Good dog!" she said as she handed it to him.		_____

NOW TRY THIS!

- **Write the paragraphs in the form of an autobiography of Tweed.**

Teachers' note The children could first enact the scenes and those taking the part of the dog could describe how they think Tweed felt about and made sense of each situation. See Introduction page 5 for useful stories to read.

100% New Developing Literacy
Creating and Shaping Texts:
Ages 10–11
© A & C BLACK

- **Compare the two versions of the passage from a biography.**
- **Say what each writer thinks about the person, and how you can tell.**

They always kept the best table for him – the one in the window, with views across the square. Usually three or four men would join him for lunch – no-one knew who they were. The paparazzi never photographed them.

Seeming more interested in his friends than in the food, he would order a salad, a glass of water and perhaps some fruit.

Other lunchers' gaze would be drawn to this dark-haired, olive-skinned man enjoying the company of his friends. Sometimes they caught his glance and he would give them a friendly smile.

_____
_____
_____
_____
_____
_____
_____
_____
_____

He always expected the best table – the one in the bay window, with views across the square. Usually he brought three or four hangers-on for lunch – ordinary-looking, unknown men, so that he would stand out: the paparazzi would photograph him.

He knew how to look more interested in his captive audience than in the food. He would pick at a salad, sip water and fiddle with some fruit – mindful of his "Mr Healthy" image.

Other lunchers tried not to stare at the orange suntan and dyed black hair. They watched as he enjoyed the attention of his audience. Sometimes they caught his glance and he would smile with satisfaction.

_____
_____
_____
_____
_____
_____
_____
_____
_____
_____

NOW TRY THIS!

- **Rewrite the passage, giving only the facts.**

Teachers' note Read the first sentence of each passage with the children and ask them what it tells them about the person. Ask them to focus on the differences: the different impressions created by 'they always kept the best table for her' and 'she always expected the best table'. Ask them to think about the connotations of words such as *hangers-on*.

100% New Developing Literacy
Creating and Shaping Texts:
Ages 10–11
© A & C BLACK

37

Same life – different views: 2

- **Write a passage for a biography about someone famous.**
- **Use language that will make readers admire the person.**
- **Rewrite the paragraph, changing the language so that readers will not think well of the person.**

Add other words and phrases.

Name of person _____

☺ _____
_____
_____
_____
_____
_____
_____
_____

☹ _____
_____
_____
_____
_____
_____
_____
_____
_____

Useful words
accepted, took
asked
gazed, glanced, looked
grinned, laughed, smiled
stepped, strolled, walked
friendly, funny, pleasant, serene, unassuming
bravely, calmly, firmly, gently, pleasantly, politely

_____
_____
_____
_____

Useful words
demanded
eyed, gawped, glared, stared, leered, smirked
grabbed, grasped, snatched
minced, sauntered, swaggered, strutted
pretentious, snobbish
nastily, unpleasantly

_____
_____

NOW TRY THIS!

- **Reread both passages.**
- **Edit and improve them.**

Think about the effects created by your choice of words. Can you think of more effective language?

Teachers' note The children should first have completed page 37. It is useful for them to read newspaper articles about celebrities and to notice how the writers use language to communicate their views of them. Encourage them to use a thesaurus to find alternatives for the words they first think of and to consider the different shades of meaning.

100% New Developing Literacy
Creating and Shaping Texts:
Ages 10–11
© A & C BLACK

Notes to news

- **Write a report for a local newspaper using the reporter's notes.**

Use quotations to add impact.

Grabbs Bank, Town Road, Silton broken into yesterday approx 7am. Broke into 'QuickPrint' next door (printers – wedding invitations, cards, etc). Mary Font, 37, who runs shop had call from police to say there had been break-in. Thieves used cutting equipment to cut through thru' rear wall into bank. Tried to open safe & force open cash machine. Damaged electricity supply & pulled down display boards. Mrs Font said didn't know at first that break-in was to do with cash machine but later realised that cash machine had been smeared with mud at weekend to stop people using it. Said whole shop smelled of smoke and there were abandoned pick axe handles and gas canisters. Thieves fled empty-handed when cutting equipment sparked off fire. Didn't get into cash machine but, Mrs Font said, wrecked all her stock, including all her hand-made invitation cards. Said luckily she knows builder who could fix wall. Said the bank was no longer staffed – just cash machines – and would talk to Grabbs' bosses about future security arrangements. No-one available to comment from Grabbs.

Headline _____

Introduction _____

_____

_____

The story _____

_____

_____

_____

_____

_____

_____

Ending _____

_____

Say **what** the story is about. Capture readers' interest with a dynamic sentence.

Tell readers **what** happened, **where**, **how** and **when**.

Write briefly. Use quotations.

Write active sentences.

End with a comment.

NOW TRY THIS!

- **Edit your story. Try changing the order of the sentences.**

Teachers' note First read news reports from a local newspaper with the children and draw their attention to the important features. See the Introduction on page 8 for more detail on these.

100% New Developing Literacy
Creating and Shaping Texts:
Ages 10–11
© A & C BLACK

Radio news

- **Plan and write a radio news report about something that has happened at your school or in the local area.**
- **Make it suitable for younger children at your school.**

Use simple language: short sentences, active verbs, simple vocabulary. Explain any difficult or technical terms.

What happened	Where
	Who
	When
What people said about it (who, why)	

Introduction _____

_____

The story _____

_____

_____

_____

Ending _____

_____

Tell readers **what** happened, **where**, **how** and **when**.

Keep it brief. Use one or two quotations.

End with a comment.

NOW TRY THIS!

- **Practise reading your article aloud with a friend.**
- **Use different tones of voice, change the pace and volume.**
- **Change any parts that are difficult to read.**

Teachers' note Ask the children about the similarities and differences between a radio and a newspaper report. Note that both use quotations and that in a radio report the different voices of the interviewer and interviewee add interest. Emphasise the need for description in a radio report, since photographs, diagrams and maps cannot be used.

100% New Developing Literacy
Creating and Shaping Texts:
Ages 10–11
© A & C BLACK

News evaluation

- **Use this page to evaluate your radio news report.**

> Think about how people answered and what you found out.

Interview questions

The best questions we asked	What made them good
_____	_____
_____	_____
_____	_____
_____	_____
_____	_____

How well the report answered the key questions: *What? Who? Where? When? How? Why?*

_____

_____

> Explain your answers.

_____

_____

How well we used language

How easy was the report to understand? _____

_____

How well did you explain unusual words or technical terms? _____

_____

How interesting was the language? _____

_____

How well did you use your voices? _____

> Think about tone of voice, speaking clearly, and changing pace and volume.

_____

_____

NOW TRY THIS!

- **Use your evaluation to help you to edit the recorded programme.**

Teachers' note Refer to the criteria used for planning interview questions for a radio report so that the children can apply these to their report when they play it back. Evaluate how well each of the important questions (*What? When? Where? Who? How? Why?*) was answered by the report. Discuss the presentational features in the final section of the evaluation.

**100% New Developing Literacy
Creating and Shaping Texts:
Ages 10–11**
© A & C BLACK

News editor

- **Edit this news article.**
- **Use powerful verbs and interesting adjectives and adverbs.**
- **Write any new text in the margin.**

Use a colour that will show up well: for example, red.

Useful symbols

	insert
	delete
⊙	full stop (the circle makes it show up)
	indent line
	remove indent
	new line

A lot of the Pentham Under-11 League football matches were put off until another date this weekend. This happened because there had been a lot of snow and the pitches were covered by snow. Gateway's pitch and Cargill's pitch were both under 30 centimetres of snow.

Only one of the twelve matches that was played. The only match that were played was Rodley v Minedale Bears. Rodley goalkeeper Sally Holder helped Rodley to avoid relegation with three fine saves. These were in the second half She saved three cracking shots by Ali Khan, James Boote and Anna Header. Gemma Scorer headed in the only goal of the match she plays for Rodley. The goal came from a fine pass from the right wing. It was Andy Cross who kicked it from about 2 metres.

Jenny Tacklit, the captain of Rodley said, "It was a close game with good shots from both teams Sally saved the game for us, though.

NOW TRY THIS!

- **What other information do you think the article should give?**
- **Write your suggestions in the form of an email to the sports reporter.**

Teachers' note The children should make notes about how the article can be improved, perhaps by: changing the order of sentences, shortening sentences, replacing words and altering punctuation. Introduce the proofreading symbols shown in the key above and demonstrate how to use them (see Introduction page 9).

100% New Developing Literacy Creating and Shaping Texts: Ages 10–11
© A & C BLACK

Sports reporter

- **Write a report about a school sports event.**
- **Use interesting language to make readers want to read it.**

What was the event? Where?

Headline

Introduction

_____

_____

_____

_____

What sport? Who: which group(s) of people took part? When? Where?

Story

_____

_____

_____

_____

What were the main events? How did they happen? Why? What interesting, but less important observations did you make? What did those taking part say?

_____

_____

_____

_____

_____

Summary

_____

_____

_____

What did you think of the event?

NOW TRY THIS!

- **Rewrite your report as a script for an 'on-the-spot' radio commentary.**
- **Use the present tense.**

Teachers' note The children should make a note of useful words and phrases in sports reports in newspapers and collect examples of the ways sports reporters add excitement to their reports. Discuss the structure of the reports: they make the chronological order of events clear to the reader, although maintaining interest by not writing in a list-like way.

100% New Developing Literacy Creating and Shaping Texts: Ages 10–11 © A & C BLACK

Planners' point of view

- **Rewrite this unbiased report from the point of view of the energy company.**
- **Use language that suggests that their view is the sensible one and that the villagers are wrong.**
- **Write a headline that shows bias towards the energy company.**

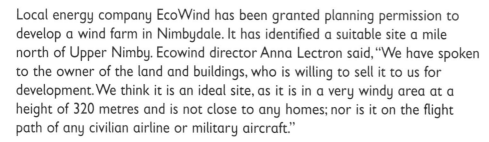

Useful words and phrases

backward-looking
behind the times
betrayed
blot on the landscape
clean energy
decrepit
derelict
dilapidated
disgrace
enhance
enrich
excellent
eyesore
forward-thinking
graceful
grasped
harnessing natural resources
immaculate
impressive
innovative
latest
old-fashioned
opportunity
perfect
profiteering
progressive
sleek
spectacular
stick-in-the-mud
superb
super-efficient
ugly
ultra-clean
ultra-modern

Local energy company EcoWind has been granted planning permission to develop a wind farm in Nimbydale. It has identified a suitable site a mile north of Upper Nimby. Ecowind director Anna Lectron said, "We have spoken to the owner of the land and buildings, who is willing to sell it to us for development. We think it is an ideal site, as it is in a very windy area at a height of 320 metres and is not close to any homes; nor is it on the flight path of any civilian airline or military aircraft."

Farmers Esa and Ima Grasper want to retire. They cannot afford to keep their farm buildings in good repair: "This will improve the view for our neighbours in Upper Nimby and for tourists," said Mrs Grasper, 79. "They will no longer have to look at them."

Nimbydale council leader Bill Ditupp said he thought that this was an ideal opportunity for the area to meet its 'Green Targets' for energy: "We have to make the most of our area's natural resources."

Residents of Upper Nimby opposed the plan because, they said, it would spoil the area's natural beauty. Rosa Greens, 34, said, "It all comes down to money, not care for the environment – money for the Graspers and money for EcoWind. I shall not comment on the council's gains."

Her next-door neighbour Juno Watt, 76, said, "This is a beautiful village with a beautiful view. All that is to change. It is a quiet area; now it will be noisy – first with construction traffic and then with the noise of the turbines."

Residents of Upper Nimby plan to appeal against the council's decision: "We will not accept this without a fight," said Hugh Punch, 64.

"Local residents were consulted during the planning review," said Anna Lectron. "EcoWind went through all the proper legal procedures. Now we are looking forward to making progress at the site."

NOW TRY THIS!

- **Rewrite the article from the villagers' viewpoint.**

Teachers' note Point out the difference between writing in a biased way and presenting the views of others in a balanced way. Model how the bias of the report would change by altering a few words and phrases in the first sentence: for example, 'develop a wind farm that will harness the natural resources of Nimbydale to provide clean energy'.

100% New Developing Literacy
Creating and Shaping Texts:
Ages 10–11
© A & C BLACK

Cooking for all

Do you think it should be compulsory for all children to be taught to cook at school? **Yes/No**

- **Collect evidence to support your view.**
- **Make notes.**
- **Quote some people and texts.**

The headings on the chart will help.

> Interview teachers, including your headteacher.

> Use leaflets from supermarkets and health centres.

> Use the Internet.

> Interview experts on health and cooking.

Health	Money
School timetable	Employment
Growing up	Enjoyment

NOW TRY THIS!

- **Write sentences from your notes.**

Teachers' note Ask the children to think about the question and to write their own individual opinions. They should then look for evidence to support them. Point out that during this process they could change their minds, based on the evidence they find. See Introduction page 9 for useful sources of information.

**100% New Developing Literacy
Creating and Shaping Texts:
Ages 10–11**
© A & C BLACK

To cook or not to cook

- **Write an argument to persuade others about whether cookery lessons should be compulsory for all children.**

I am convinced that _____

_____

According to _____

_____

_____

This is supported by _____

_____

_____

Also _____

_____

_____

_____

_____

_____

Finally _____

_____

_____

In conclusion _____

_____

_____

NOW TRY THIS!

- **Listen to others' opinions.**
- **Make a note of anything they say that might make you change your mind or make others with the same view change their minds.**

Teachers' note The children should have researched the topic (see page 45) so that they can support their views with evidence. You could model the difference between sentences composed to give information and those composed in order to persuade by emphasising persuasive words and phrases, such as *certainly, surely, without doubt*.

100% New Developing Literacy
Creating and Shaping Texts:
Ages 10–11
© A & C BLACK

Sum it up

- Listen to others presenting opposite views about an issue.
- Write notes about each side of the argument.
- Draw a conclusion.

The issue _____

View 1		View 2	
Points made	My comments	Points made	My comments

My conclusion is that _____

This is because _____

100% New Developing Literacy
Creating and Shaping Texts:
Ages 10–11
© A & C BLACK

NOW TRY THIS!

- Explain why one of the points in the argument is more important than the others.

I think that…

Teachers' note Explain that an argument has more than one side and that the children should listen to these and make notes so that they can write a balanced summary. Topics could be: cooking in schools (see pages 45–46); pets in public places, a local concern (relate to geography or citizenship) such as the building of a bypass or a new supermarket.

Question it

- **Write questions that listeners who disagree with the speaker might ask.**

There should be a law banning the manufacture of mini planes that people can fly around as if they were airborne cars. Imagine the danger to members of the public if people were allowed to fly around our villages, towns and cities in these contraptions. However light they were in weight, they could surely harm any buildings they collided with. What if they crashed into someone's bedroom or living room window (or the window of any other room)?

Mid-air collisions would certainly happen once the air filled up with these dangerous machines. Anyone unfortunate enough to be below would surely be injured, or even killed. The police have a hard enough job trying to control traffic on the ground – let alone jetting around above our heads.

Furthermore, I shudder to think about the chaos these monsters would cause when they landed on the streets or tried to park.

No sensible person would support this perilous development. It should be banned.

NOW TRY THIS!

- **Find out more about the topic.**
- **Write answers to your questions.**

Teachers' note What might happen if people could buy tiny planes to use like cars? Consider the advantages and disadvantages and write questions to ask the speaker, who opposes them. Half a group could ask questions and the other half could answer them. Encourage them to act as 'devil's advocate' in order to draw out ideas.

100% New Developing Literacy
Creating and Shaping Texts:
Ages 10–11
© A & C BLACK

Class debate

- **Write a summary of a class debate.**
- **Write your conclusion.**

Listen to different points of view.

Challenge the speakers to give evidence.

Ask questions to find out more.

The question for the debate _____
_____

My summary

_____
_____
_____
_____
_____
_____
_____
_____
_____
_____
_____
_____
_____
_____

In conclusion _____
_____
_____
_____
_____

Word-bank

all in all
all the same
although
but
certainly
clearly
considering
despite
even if
even so
even though
evidently
finally
however
in case
in spite of the fact that
it could be argued
just the same
maybe
naturally
no doubt
nonetheless
of course
obviously
on the one hand
on the other hand
perhaps
possibly
so
still
supposing
surely
therefore
though
thus
while
whilst
yet

NOW TRY THIS!

- **With a partner, evaluate the debate.**
How clearly did the speakers make their points?
How well did they support them with evidence?

Teachers' note A new topic could be introduced or this activity could be linked to a previous topic that has been discussed (see pages 46–48). Remind the children that their task is to present a balanced summary of the discussion and not a persuasive argument.

**100% New Developing Literacy
Creating and Shaping Texts:
Ages 10–11**
© A & C BLACK

Make it formal

- **Rewrite Millie's tour to the school garden as a part of a leaflet for visitors.**
- **Write in the third person.**
- **Use more formal language: more formal vocabulary, some passive verbs, no contractions, no slang.**

We got a lot of stuff from neighbours, like this old gate. We liked it so we painted it blue 'cos someone gave us a load of blue paint and we like blue.

There's a gravel path because that doesn't get slippery when it's wet. That little bit of path goes to a seat under the beech tree where it's shady. A man bought it for the school and put a plaque that says Mrs Sonja Patel on it because she was his wife and she used to be a teacher here but she died.

That patch is full of heathers. They have blue and purple and pink flowers in the autumn and they have leaves all the time.

We've got all kinds of lichens and mosses on that little wall. We measure each year to see how much they've spread.

That's a beech hedge along the west side. It still has a lot of leaves in the winter and it shelters the garden.

We've put hyacinths in clumps under the trees in the north side to look nice. They smell nice, too.

_____

_____

_____

_____

_____

_____

_____

_____

_____

_____

_____

Teachers' note Invite a volunteer to give another child (acting as a newcomer) a tour of the classroom. Then invite him or her to repeat this for an 'adult visitor' (see Introduction page 10). Ask how the two tours were different, and why. Focus on the language, although tone of voice and overall demeanour will make a difference.

100% New Developing Literacy
Creating and Shaping Texts:
Ages 10–11
© A & C BLACK

Guide to Stadium School: 1

- **Plan an interactive guide to Stadium school.**
- **Use hyperlinks to add information.**
- **Make notes about what to write or what pictures to use in each layer.**

The notes for the introduction have been written for you.

Introduction

Purpose of school

How pupils are selected (who they are, their families)

Brief description of building and setting

Instructions for using interactive guide (how to use hyperlinks to find out more)

Site guide (contents headings for hyperlinks)

Staff

House system

Essential equipment

Curriculum

Uniform

Rules

NOW TRY THIS!

- **Write the introduction.**
- **Use formal language.**

I wonder if Stadium School is like Hogwarts?

Teachers' note They could begin by making notes about a fictional school from memory and then skim the books to refresh their memories and find out more. After completing this page they could allocate a section of the guide to each member of their group. Continued on page 52.

**100% New Developing Literacy
Creating and Shaping Texts:
Ages 10–11
© A & C BLACK**

Guide to Stadium School: 2

- **Share the tasks of writing an interactive guide to Stadium School.**
- **Tick your section:**

Work in a group of six.

Staff		Curriculum		House system		Uniform		Essential equipment		Rules	

- **Write the introduction to your section.**
- **Plan some hyperlinks.**
- **Write headings and notes for the hyperlinks.**

Remember to use formal language.

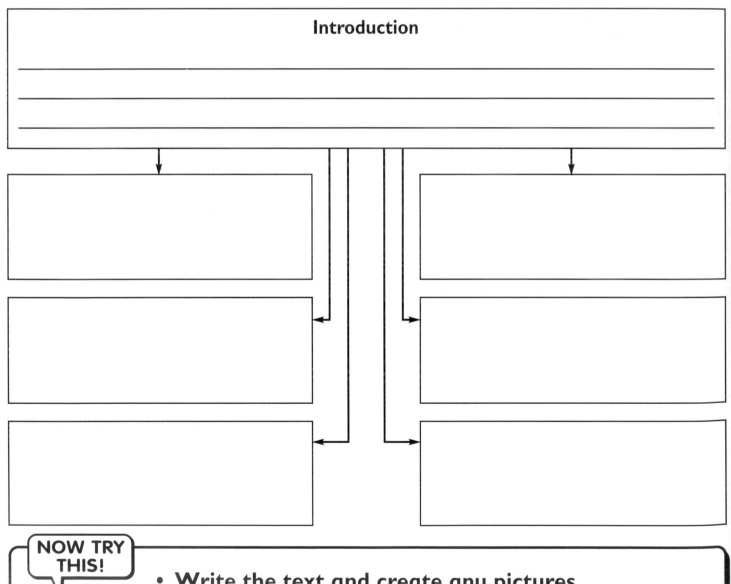

Introduction

_____

_____

_____

NOW TRY THIS!

- **Write the text and create any pictures for the hyperlinks.**

Teachers' note Continued from page 51. Ask the children to write sentences for this introduction based on their notes. Remind them that language should be fairly formal (no slang, no contractions, precise vocabulary). They can organise their notes from page 51 into sections to expand using hyperlinks (see Introduction page 10).

100% New Developing Literacy
Creating and Shaping Texts:
Ages 10–11
© A & C BLACK

52

Formal notice

- **Write a notice to tell people the conditions they agree to when they buy a theatre ticket.**
- **Use the information in the notes.**

Use formal language. The first paragraph has been started for you.

Can't have money back for ticket if not used

Must show whole ticket

If book online bring receipt

If ticket badly damaged might not be let in

No talking during play

No hats in theatre – block people's view

Must sit down no later than 5 mins before start when lights go off until interval

If late will be told not to go in but wait for end of scene

No glasses in auditorium

No rustling papers while play is on

We'll ring a bell 3 mins before interval ends to warn you

Exits and toilets have lit-up signs

Formal word-bank

advise	performance
arrive	present
audience	produce
conversation	prohibited
duration	refund
during	refuse
enter	requested
entire	required
entrance	reservations
headgear	seated
illuminated	sounded
lighting	theatre-goers
obstruct	vision

Conditions of ticket sales and attendance

Purchasers of tickets are advised that no refunds will be available on unused tickets. _____

_____

_____

_____

_____

_____

_____

NOW TRY THIS!

- **Write the conditions in simple language for someone who does not speak English.**

Teachers' note Ask the children to read the notes about theatre tickets and to rate them on a scale of formality from 1 to 5 (where 5 is very formal). Invite feedback. They should be able to justify their judgements. Ask them to compare the first notes with the first sentence in the conditions and to comment on what makes the language become more formal.

100% New Developing Literacy
Creating and Shaping Texts:
Ages 10–11
© A & C BLACK

Voice-over

- **Write a voice-over for a virtual tour of a place you know.**
- **Write notes about what will be on the screen for each image.**
- **Write what you will say and record for each image.**

Use impersonal language.

Personal language	Impersonal language
Speaking directly to the listener: You can see the mountains…	Speaking indirectly to the listener: Viewers can see the mountains…
Active verbs: Look at the mountains…	Passive verbs: The mountains can be seen…
First person: I am going to show…	Third person: This tour shows…

Place _____

Image	Image on screen	Voice-over
1		
2		
3		
4		

NOW TRY THIS!

- **Record your voice-over.**
- **Listen to it with a friend and edit it.**

Do I really sound like that?

Teachers' note The children can choose the four key features of their chosen site and make notes about what to show on screen and what to say in the voice-over. This might involve some research during a visit to the site or from leaflets, books or the Internet. Consider that their audience is unknown so the language should be impersonal.

100% New Developing Literacy
Creating and Shaping Texts:
Ages 10–11
© A & C BLACK

Getting personal

- **Imagine the thunderstorm is a person.**
  How does the person feel?
  What is he or she doing?
  What kind of sounds is he or she making?
- **Make notes in the flashes.**

If possible, watch a video of a thunderstorm.

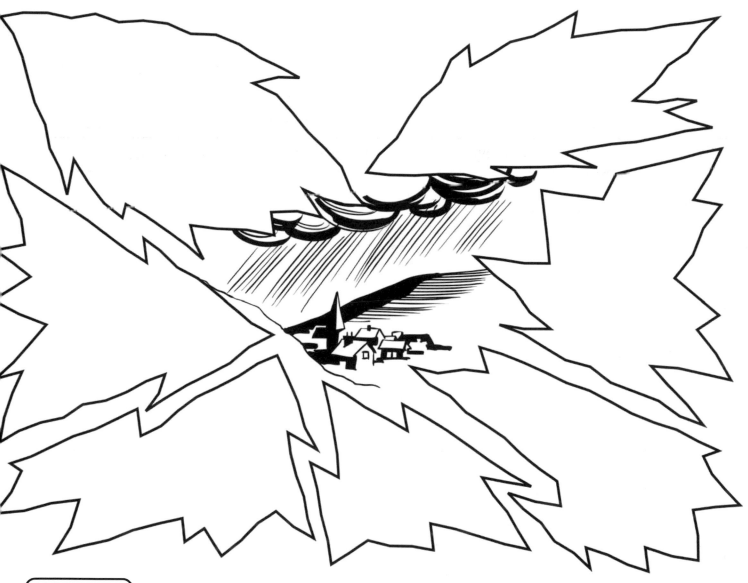

NOW TRY THIS!

- **Choose the two notes you think best personify the storm.**
- **Write them in lines of poetry to create the image and atmosphere of the storm.**

Do not try to make the lines rhyme, unless you come across rhymes that help to create the atmosphere.

Teachers' note Read several poems that feature personification and encourage appreciation of the powerful effects it can have in creating an image. Watch a short film together of a thunderstorm and then suggest words to describe it and to recount what happens. Imagine the storm as a person: say what he or she looks like, does and says.

100% New Developing Literacy Creating and Shaping Texts: Ages 10–11
© A & C BLACK

Traffic personified

- **Watch traffic on a webcam.**
**Try to observe some stationary traffic, some
moving slowly and some moving faster.
Imagine the throb of the traffic
as if it is someone's heartbeat.**
- **Make notes about your ideas.**
- **Write a short poem that
creates an image of the traffic.**
- **Use personification.**

> What are the heartbeat and breathing like of someone who is still, and then moving at different speeds?

> What kinds of human movement does traffic make you think of?

Title _____

_____

_____

_____

_____

_____

_____

_____

_____

_____

_____

_____

_____

Notes

pulsing

pushing a path

pushing through clogged veins

_____

_____

_____

_____

_____

_____

_____

_____

_____

_____

_____

NOW TRY THIS!

- **Read your poem aloud and think about the
image you want.
How well does the poem do this?**
- **Make changes to create this image.**

Teachers' note Introduce the idea of the traffic and roads as part of a giant. Ask what the roads
could be (perhaps arteries and veins) and what the vehicles could be (perhaps material carried
along in the bloodstream – for example, waste products like carbon dioxide being taken back to
the lungs). The children could research this.

100% New Developing Literacy
Creating and Shaping Texts:
Ages 10–11
© A & C BLACK

Images of people

If these fruits were people, what would they be like?
Who might they be?

- Draw the people.
- Write any words or phrases you can think of to create an image of the person.

Think of famous people, or people you know.

NOW TRY THIS!

- Write a verse about one of the people.

Teachers' note Begin by discussing the qualities of fruits that could be applied to people and listing adjectives that could describe both fruit and people (sometimes literally for a fruit and figuratively for a person): round, long, fat, broad, soft, sweet, prickly. The children could think of a fruit's outline that someone reminds them of.

**100% New Developing Literacy
Creating and Shaping Texts:
Ages 10–11**
© A & C BLACK

De-personified

- **Use non-living images to create images of people.**

What do they look like?

What personal characteristics do they have?

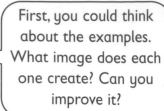

First, you could think about the examples. What image does each one create? Can you improve it?

Example:
A puff of a girl – quiet and pleasant
But nothing within
A puff of air that came and went
Leaving no mark.

Example:
A deep pool, dark and still
That seemed to have existed for all time
Brewing wise words.

1 A violent young man _____
_____
_____
_____
_____
_____
_____

2 An old man whose body is weak but his mind is strong
_____
_____
_____
_____
_____
_____

3 A baby – small and vulnerable, needing to be cared for
_____
_____
_____
_____
_____

4 A very unhappy bully
_____
_____
_____
_____
_____
_____

NOW TRY THIS!

- **Choose one of the images to develop into a poem about the person.**

Teachers' note Show photographs of people (perhaps use an interactive whiteboard for recording the children's ideas for words to describe them). Ask for suggestions of non-living things to create a verbal image of the people: they should focus on the most obvious impressions, such as height, girth, shape, posture, evil, smugness, happiness.

100% New Developing Literacy
Creating and Shaping Texts:
Ages 10–11
© A & C BLACK

Wacky poem

- **Read the poem aloud with a friend.**
- **Explain what makes it funny.**

_____
_____
_____
_____
_____

- **Use the wacky poem cards to help you to write a funny poem that has a surprise at the end.**
- **Try out your ideas first on the notepad.**

Out of Sight

"Cheer up mate"
shouted the jolly roadsweeper
to the longfaced passerby
And bending down
lifted up a corner
of the tarmac
and swept away the dust.

Roger McGough

Title _____

'_____,'

shouted the _____

to the longfaced passerby

and _____

_____

_____

and _____

_____

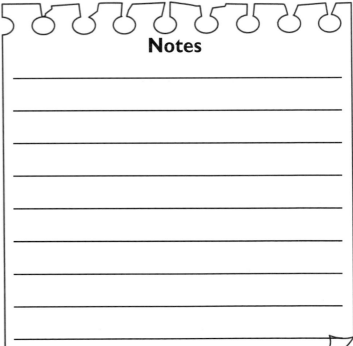

Notes

 **NOW TRY THIS!**

- **Edit and polish your poem. You could think of different words to replace these:**

| shouted | longfaced | passerby |

Teachers' note Before giving out copies of this page, read the first four lines of the poem and ask the children to suggest what might come next. Read the rest of it. This should surprise the children. Some of them might be able to think up their own ideas for a wacky poem but most will need help from the suggestions on the wacky poem cards (page 60).

**100% New Developing Literacy
Creating and Shaping Texts:
Ages 10–11
© A & C BLACK**

Wacky poem cards

 The hairdresser

 The window cleaner

 The postman

 The gardener

 The baker

 The homeless person

 The bin man

 The lollipop lady

 The traffic warden

 The cashier

 The farmer

 The dentist

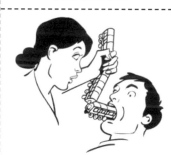

Teachers' note Use these with page 59. The children could begin by pairing the characters with the ideas cards and making up lines for a poem with a partner. Ask them to write about something ordinary and everyday in the first three or four lines and then introduce a surprise.

60

100% New Developing Literacy
Creating and Shaping Texts:
Ages 10–11
© A & C BLACK

Abandoned: 1

- **Use this page to organise your research for a poem about abandoned dogs.**

Use the Internet.

Add other questions of your own.

Note down powerful quotations from people and websites.

Facts I know about abandoned dogs	Questions	Answers
	Are any breeds abandoned more often than others? Why?	
	How do abandoned dogs behave towards people and towards other dogs? What does their behaviour show about how they feel?	
	What happens to dogs found abandoned?	

NOW TRY THIS!

What do you think abandoned dogs might say if they could speak?
- **Write your ideas.**

Teachers' note Discuss what the children know about abandoned dogs and research the topic with the help of questions of their own and finding the answers. Include their responses to what they find out: for example, feeling pity for the dogs and for dog owners unable to care of their pets, anger at cruelty, support for dog welfare charities.

100% New Developing Literacy
Creating and Shaping Texts:
Ages 10–11
© A & C BLACK

61

Abandoned: 2

- In the speech bubbles, write what the abandoned dog might be thinking. Include some questions.

Write in the first person. Use direct language that talks to the reader or listener (use 'you').

- Use this to help you to write a monologue for an abandoned dog.

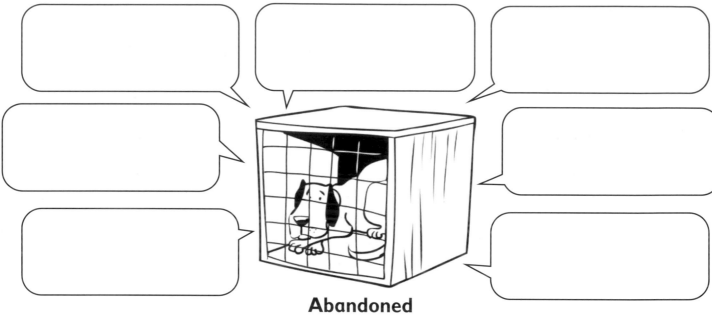

Abandoned

NOW TRY THIS!

- **Read your poem aloud.**
- **Underline any words or phrases you can improve.**

Think about powerful verbs and interesting adjectives. Think about the sounds of the words.

Teachers' note The children should first have researched abandoned dogs, laws about cruelty to animals, the duty of caring for them and the charities that care for them. Ask them to imagine they are an abandoned dog. Clarify that a monologue is a form of poem in this case, as both terms are used.

100% New Developing Literacy Creating and Shaping Texts: Ages 10–11
© A & C BLACK

The last passenger pigeon

How do you feel about the passenger pigeon?
- ## Make notes to help you to write a poem about it.

You might feel sad.

You might feel angry.

You might think it does not matter.

You might feel glad.

DEDICATED
TO THE LAST WISCONSIN
PASSENGER PIGEON
SHOT AT BABCOCK, SEPT 1899
THIS SPECIES BECAME
EXTINCT
THROUGH THE AVARICE AND
THOUGHTLESSNESS OF MAN

This monument stands in Wyalusung National Park, Wisconsin. There were once billions of passenger pigeons in North America. They had some natural predators: hawks, owls, eagles, weasels, skunks and a few tree snakes and Native Americans caught them in large nets, for food. The early settlers copied them, but no-one worried about the birds because of their vast numbers.

Settlers cut down forests that provided the food for the pigeons (beechnuts, acorns, other nuts and berries) and trappers began to catch them to supply the new cities of the United States with cheap meat. The new railways helped to transport them quickly and, by 1855, 300,000 pigeons were being sent to New York each year.

The birds became so rare that the Cincinnati Zoo tried to breed them but on 1 September, 1914 the last one, Martha, was found dead at the bottom of her cage. Her body was preserved and can still be seen in the National Museum of Natural History in Washington DC.

Notes

Teachers' note Tell the children that they are going to prepare their ideas for a poem about the passenger pigeon, beginning with the facts and then considering how they feel about the extinction of these birds. This could be linked with work on arguments, in which they write notes for a dialogue between people with different views.

100% New Developing Literacy
Creating and Shaping Texts:
Ages 10–11
© A & C BLACK

63

Passenger pigeon rap

- **Work in a group that feels the same way about the last passenger pigeon.**
- **Try out ideas for a rap about it.**
- **Choose words that express how you feel.**
- **Write your rap.**

> The word-and-phrase-bank will help. You could add some of your own.

Word-and-phrase-bank

Angry	**Sad**	**Couldn't care**	**Glad**
dead bird, dead breed feathers falling netted, hunted, trapped in nets	the last bird – someone cared lonely alone sole survivor	just a bird – who cared? what a fuss when it bit the dust	perish the pest vanished vermin germ-spreading muck dropping good riddance, glad riddance

---

Passenger pigeon rap

_____

_____

_____

_____

_____

_____

_____

_____

_____

_____

> Use a thesaurus to find powerful verbs and expressive adjectives.

> Think about the nouns you use. Look for others that might express your feelings better.

> You could include some well-chosen adverbs.

NOW TRY THIS!

- **Perform your rap with your group.**
- **Discuss it and try out any changes you think will help.**

Teachers' note Remind the children that many raps are written in direct language as if talking to someone or as a monologue. Ask what the children would like to say to the Native Americans, the European settlers or shooters who killed the passenger pigeons, the people who enjoyed eating them in restaurants or Martha (the last passenger pigeon).

100% New Developing Literacy
Creating and Shaping Texts:
Ages 10–11
© A & C BLACK